# Starfish on the Beach

Tom and Lindy Schneider

Text Copyright © 2012 by Tom and Lindy Schneider
Illustrations Copyright © 2012 by Lindy Schneider

All rights reserved. No part of this publication may be reproduced in whole or in part, or stored in a retrieval system, or transmitted in any form or by any means, electronic, mechanical, photocopying, recording or otherwise, without written permission of the publisher. For information regarding permission, write to Peaks Publishing.
www.PeaksPublishing.com

Starfish on the Beach was inspired by The Star Thrower by Loren Eiseley.

Schneider, Tom and Lindy
Starfish on the Beach

Summary: A mom and daughter find starfish on the beach drying in the sun. They find they can't save them all but they can make a difference for some of them.
1) Children's Stories - American [1. Starfish - fiction  2. Mother and Daughter - fiction]
ISBN: 978-0-9840385-0-3

Book design by Aubrey Blankenship

Printed in the U.S.A.
Published by Peaks Publishing

# Starfish on the Beach

To all those who give of their time and money to make a difference in the life of a little one. — Tom

To Jeremy, Liz, Aubrey, Brandon, Cavin, Ryan, Karen, Susan and Jean for always believing in our ability to make a difference. — Lindy

One afternoon on a sparkling, sandy beach a mother and her daughter were picking up sea shells.

The tide was out so they found many treasures.

"Momma, put this in your bag, please," said the little girl and she held up a pretty pink, striped shell. Momma carried a bag for collecting such things.

Momma and Sandy walked along the shoreline making footprints side by side.

Suddenly Sandy stopped. She saw something that was bigger than a sea shell.

Sandy ran ahead for a closer look.

"Look, Momma," said Sandy, "there are stars on the beach!"

Momma looked too. "You found some starfish. They usually hide in the cool water."

"Poor starfish," said Sandy. "The sun is cooking them!"

"The tide will come back in soon and they will be alright," said Momma.

Little Sandy was not so sure. Without a word, she picked up one crusty starfish after another and tossed them into the refreshing waves.

Momma watched for a while. "You can't save them all," she said.

"I know," said Sandy and she picked up two more starfish and tossed them into the water.

The shore stretched on forever and the starfish polka-dotted the beach as far as they could see.

"Momma, could you help me?" asked Sandy.

So Momma helped rescue the starfish until a wave of sadness washed over her heart.

"There are so many starfish that need help," said Momma. "I don't think we're making much of a difference here."

Little Sandy thought for a moment and then picked up one more starfish and tossed it into the rolling waves.

She smiled as she ran back to Momma. "I made a difference for that one," she said.

Momma smiled and said, "Yes, you did!"

## The Amazing Starfish!

The starfish is not really a star because it isn't found in the sky, and it isn't really a fish because it doesn't swim! Marine scientists want to rename it a sea star. It is an echinoderm which is a sea animal with spines on its skin. It is in the same family as a sand dollar which, by the way, is not made of sand and it is not a dollar. Although the starfish doesn't swim, it can crawl, climb and hold onto rocks very tightly.

Most starfish have five arms, but some kinds of starfish can have as many as 40 arms! (Go back through Starfish on the Beach and see if you can find the starfish that has 6 arms.) The underside of each arm is covered with tube feet. On the end of each tube foot is a little sucker that helps the animal move and hold onto things. A starfish breathes through its tube feet and through breathing tubes all over its body. The breathing tubes act like gills on a fish, removing the oxygen and sending it through the starfish's whole system.

The starfish does not have a nose, or eyes, or blood or a brain! It does, however, have eyespots on the tip of each arm. With these it can see light and dark and notice something moving around it.

The mouth of the starfish is in the middle of its belly. To eat clams and oysters, its favorite foods, the starfish grabs hold of the shellfish and pulls the shell open by using its tube feet suckers. Then the starfish turns its stomach inside out and pushes it into the shell to digest the fish! When it's done, the starfish pulls its stomach back inside its body. Its bony skin protects it from most enemies, but if a fish bites off an arm, the starfish will grow the arm right back in just a few months!

See what it is like to be a starfish. First, close your eyes, then have someone turn the lights off and on several times before stopping. Can you tell if the light is on without opening your eyes? A starfish could. Can you open your lunchbox with your feet? A starfish opens its "lunchbox" with its feet everyday! Finally, take a deep breath. Now do it again and breathe with your feet. Can you do it? A starfish can!

Note to teachers and parents: For other fun starfish resources go to www.StarfishStory.com.

You make a difference!

## About the Authors

Tom & Lindy Schneider have been writing professionally for many years with their work appearing in corporate pieces, magazines and books. They have worked with children for over 20 years and together Tom and Lindy won the National Excellence in Education Award for a Young Writers Program they developed for K through 12 students. Tom was twice nominated for the Golden Apple Award for Excellence in Education for Washington State. They have also presented workshops to educators conferences in many different states.

As an illustrator, Lindy's artwork has appeared in over 500 different venues and has been purchased by many national corporations and magazines. She has won several regional and national awards for her illustrations and design work.

For a FREE report, *Raising Tiny Super Heroes: 12 Fun Ways to Build Character and Compassion in Your Toddler*, go to www.LindysBooks.com.

If this book has inspired or blessed you in some way please let us know at www.PeaksPublishing.com.

Made in the USA
Columbia, SC
01 February 2020